CW00660971

# THE
# TAROT
## ❧ PATH TO SELF DEVELOPMENT ❧
## MICHELINE STUART

SHAMBHALA
BOULDER & LONDON
1977

SHAMBHALA PUBLICATIONS, INC.
1123 SPRUCE STREET
BOULDER, COLORADO 80302

Distributed in the United States by Random House
and in Canada by Random House of Canada Ltd.

Distributed in the Commonwealth by Routledge
& Kegan Paul Ltd., London and Henley-on-Thames.

Printed in the United States of America.

The illustrations in this book are based on the Tarot cards of the ancient Marseilles deck. These designs have been used in Europe for many centuries.

# TABLE OF CONTENTS

# INTRODUCTION

As it is truly said, the Tarot is the means of living, experiencing, and not dreaming. In this short work—short because I am giving my experience, what I have lived and from this understood where to go—I deliberately omit any explanations of the symbols of the Tarot. Enough has been written about them, and if one wants to know more, there are books available.

In approaching the Tarot, there are many levels of understanding. I am grateful for all of the intellectual research which has been done into the meaning of the symbols of the cards. By no means am I against this Tradition. On the contrary, it has been a great help, in due course, to read about it, although I appreciated more the simple naming of the symbols than the most amazing poetical flights of fancy some writings contain.

Amidst all the interpretations of the Tarot, the main theme hidden in it is the theory of man's inner evolution, given step by step, showing what one will encounter on the way and directing one where to go. All the traps and rewards are indicated. Though the task appears simple, it should not be underestimated; it is arduous and the work relentless. Only supreme effort counts. Mildness and half-heartedness will not suffice. At any time our efforts can turn into their opposites. Therefore, once having awoken to our task we must *remain awake*.

For many years the pictures on the cards remained in my heart and in my head. A sentence said by the person who originally gave me a pack of the Tarot had remained strongly imprinted in my mind and had been like the light of a star to follow. Giving me a rough explanation of the traditional meaning of the cards, she said: "As for the higher arcana, I cannot say very much. *I don't know myself enough.*"

And so, during the years of trying to work hard and enthusiastically in a school for the development of consciousness, every event (as far as I could see), every observation, gradually became a living symbol of "as above so below." From time to time I was struck by the similarity of my experience to some card in the Tarot, and said to myself, "Ah, that's what it means," until one day I had gathered enough pieces of the mysterious puzzle to see in a flash the whole picture. I realized that it was a chain in which every link fitted neatly within the next. It is said that the order of the cards has shifted a bit over the centuries: I can well see it, but it does not matter. As we have to pass through each link until the whole chain has been experienced, it is of no great account if sometimes one is experienced before the other.

In order to make an intelligible explanation of what I had seen in a glimpse, it became necessary to read the Tradition and study it intellectually. The flash showed the whole, but the details had to be worked out. As I read, I was delighted to see that all I understood was being said. The *words* were there, yet the links of the chain had not been connected, because they were not studied from the level of "knowing oneself." The formulation was from the head alone. Some of the knowledge in these writings is vast and fascinating, but always something is lacking. This is because the writing is from the author's masculine side only, the intellectual part of his mind, whereas we also have emotional and instinctive sides which need to be developed and brought together with the intellectual in order to give full understanding of the ideas. Although the Tarot clearly shows the importance played by the feminine part of our being, this aspect seems to be brushed aside or, more often than not, completely misunderstood. As long as "masculine" and "feminine" are not clearly defined and deeply perceived, they will remain separated and, consequently, will fight each other. There are signs now of the beginning of a reconciliation between the masculine and the feminine, but there is far to go and the efforts toward this are mostly chaotic and pathetic.

What I saw in the Tarot is the way to reconcile our masculine and feminine halves, but it is a long and hard way upward to return to unity. When man "fell asleep" from his Edenic state, his intuitive, feminine part was separated from him in order that "she" would not fall too low with him. From that moment misunderstanding started. She lost her intellectual skill; he lost his sensitive, intuitive skill. The "serpent of wisdom" did explain to "her" the meaning of the cosmic-divine will, but how she gave the "fruit" of her weaker understanding to him, and how he "interpreted" what he heard still have their repercussion upon us, to say the least. This is why "She" must be reinstated on her throne, with the "Book of Knowledge." She must regain her full stature by developing herself with "Him." The Tarot shows the path that the sunlight illuminates all the time. It is up to us to follow it.

Each individual must undertake to attain to his full potentiality and, ultimately, his true royalty. After that he can transcend the human condition, but not before harmonizing and balancing, completely, the feminine-masculine whole. Adam and Eve have to be reunited while *on Earth* before they can re-enter Paradise.

There are many interpretations of the Tarot because there are many levels of understanding. To grasp the "teaching" given in its fundamental message, we have to be directly involved with it. It is showing the way that can carry us through the dangers of straying and error to the development of our human nature, from our animal innocence to the opening of the sublime life. However much we know of astrology, however much we know of symbology, we shall remain at the level of "The Fool" unless we realize that no amount of knowledge, alone, will develop a practical sense in us.

So let us start humbly on our way, first relinquishing our grandiose contemplation of the cosmos. We must face our position on the ladder of being, for it is by means of this ladder that we can ascend to the level from which we come. Each rung is clearly defined and our position is clearly explained. As we are only beginners, let us start at the beginning, that is, at the bottom of the ladder.

# THE FOOL

HUMANITY IS YOUNG AND not yet mature. Therefore the Fool is represented by a young person. He is walking towards the abyss, turning his back to the light, and facing his shadow, because the sun is behind him. There certainly is light, but the darkness comprehends it not. In order to reach the threshold of the path initiating the creative process, he should be turning around to face the light, but his ignorant, human nature causes him to mistake the shadow for reality. Instead of facing the unknown of the Holy, he faces the unknown of the abyss. His animal nature, biting and kicking him, is urging him on his way. His essential garment is white, but it is covered by the dark coat of ignorance. He lives in fantasies, in imagination, subject to the hazards of life. He is passive, although convinced of the contrary, impulsive, abandoned to blind instincts. Irresponsible, incapable of directing himself, under the power of every influence, anything can happen

6

to him. He is under the law of accident without realizing it and blames life for the events he encounters and for putting him into situations which, in truth, his foolishness has attracted. He interprets everything in his own fashion, on his own level of being.

He will continue to remain like this until something happens that shocks him into facing his situation. Then he will begin to wonder about the meaning of his life and of life in general: he will begin questioning his condition and look for the answers. He will begin to see that he is immersed in the world.

This Fool *is* us. If there is to be any hope of saving ourselves from the abyss, we must first acknowledge this fact. If we remain at the level of the Fool, we continue to stay childish and immature. For the rest of our life this will be our inner condition, no matter our achievements externally, in the world.

# THE WORLD

**M**OTHER NA-
TURE IN ALL
her nakedness, con-
fronts us. Desiring to attach
us to herself, by her artifices
she has woven around us the
chain of nature, from which
we cannot escape. We are her
slaves; we belong to her. We
may or may not be happy in
this condition. In any case
we cannot do much to
change it. She rules. We
have no control over our
situation. Her laws are
stronger than we are. We
may think that we know
what we are doing, that we
are able to make decisions, that we are conscious, that
we have a will of our own, that we are our own masters:
but we are only pawns in her game. Perchance, in our
sleep-walking, we may have heard a trumpet sounding
somewhere and momentarily opened our eyes enough to
realize that we toil and suffer merely to keep alive. Not
having enough strength to remain alert, we relapse into
the embraces of Mother Nature. Thus we continue,
struggling, fighting, crying, laughing, joyous, grieving;

# THE WORLD

in brief, behaving just like human beings. Whether we have ox-earthly instincts, or lion-fiery instincts, whether we are in type like eagles, or even angelic, all these characteristics are the attributes, *on this level*, of human nature.

Two giants, pride and vanity, dominate us and are jealous of their powers if we attempt to escape them. While we are ruled by them, we shall always imagine that we are masters of our lives. Yet to become truly masters of our nature is our raison d'être: it is our birthright, the possibility latent within us. Imagining that we already are masters of ourselves, we ruin and violate our lives, destroying our foothold. If we do not awake before it is too late, we shall remain as the Fool and be precipitated into the abyss; but if we attempt to awaken and ascend the ladder of being, we shall see that, at each step upward, there is always the choice either of continuing upward, or of descending, as does the Fool.

In resolving to attempt to awaken from a state ruled over by Mother Nature and to begin the process of our inner evolution, it is very important to take into account the power of the forces that oppose our aim. In order to release ourselves from the endless cycles of suffering, the rules given from above—in the Tarot and in other esoteric teachings, as well as from the higher levels of consciousness within us—must be followed. We must never underestimate the forces of nature and their power to hold us down. We have to learn how to use these forces as a springboard, instead of being used by them. The apprenticeship is long and the way is long, but certain teachings, such as the Tarot, give precise directives.

From now onward we must take care to recognize the forces of opposition. They will be manifold, using all manner of means to keep us chained. For example, we may meet many so-called "Masters," different dubious teachings, all kinds of obstacles, diversions and worldly attractions. We shall be in danger of drowning beneath so many confusing occurrences: for the most part we shall be incapable of recognizing the tares from the wheat.

However, if our desire to improve our condition is a genuine wish to return to our source, and is not for self-aggrandizement, we will hear the trumpet blast sounded by the angel from on high.

# THE JUDGEMENT

WE DO NOT, ALL OF A SUDDEN, wake up and find ourselves balanced and free of clothing, as is shown in the picture. On the contrary, the picture is instructing us *what* to do now. We must strip off our clothing, all our mental, emotional, and physical habits, everything acquired from which we derive the erroneous ideas, suppositions, and feelings of ourselves. This is ceaseless, intense work, needing to be carried out faithfully and forever, accompanying us up the whole scale of ascent, just as the sound of a note in the musical scale continues throughout a whole octave.

Everything is linked. Unquestionably it is wrong to practice by itself what one card indicates and then, dropping it, change to the subject of the next. Each step is related and must be carried on, one to another in continual practice, becoming broader and bigger as we proceed, in order to accommodate all the work that has already been done. Thus the being is stretched. When the last

11

note, so to say, is reached, the first note is still sounding.

Only those with ears to hear and with eyes to see will grasp the meaning of this card. It is telling us to awake from our sleep, from our grave. At this stage we must discard the clothing of the natural self, our usual mental attitudes, preconceived ideas, likes and dislikes, self-complacency, aggressiveness, sentimentality, and our hates: in brief, everything that belongs to the three parts of our nature—our intellect, emotions, and instincts. We have to stand naked, purified, if we are to hear and understand the messages and directives which will be unfolded as we proceed onward.

Man and woman must be reborn in their essential nature. That is to say, they must develop their true essence, which is but a child at this stage. They have to become balanced and mature by harmonizing the minds which control their intellectual, emotional, instinctive, and moving centers. At present one of these centers is more powerful than the others. As a result our being is lopsided; our lives are largely propulsed by the predominating center at the expense of the rest of our being whose potentialities are neglected. We must start to educate these little-used centers and tame our wild, natural self.

In this card the Angel, as the positive energy above us, is making its call heard, sending the force by which the level of our being may be raised. Only at this stage of awakening can human beings receive help from above. Having transcended their male and female nature for the sake of their essential regeneration, and being torn apart no longer, but unified in their true being, they can hear the messages which are being given. Now that they are open to their own higher intellect, which was hitherto inaccessible and is an instrument far superior to the ordinary brain's sense-based faculties, they can start to understand what is demanded of them. They are lifting their arms in appeal to receive these positive energies, in prayer and submissiveness. No longer will they be enslaved to the self-will; the will from above will guide them. Now and forever they must be wakeful, alert, diligent, and enthused, lest nature's negative forces try to pull them backwards. Also let them beware that their eagerness does not turn into spiritual drunkenness or fanaticism. We must learn humility and not become excited or exalted. We must increase in understanding until only the call is heard, and we become more willing to advance further. The Fool will stay at this stage, mistaking the message for illumination.

There is yet a great way to go, and we need a vehicle to carry us.

# THE SUN

ESSENCE, WHEN IT AWAKENS AT THE age of enthusiastic adolescence, sets out on its way to the sun-spirit, sitting on the impetuous horse of desire. Once mastered, this animal energy can become useful; its great strength can carry us toward our goal. When no more seized by and at the mercy of worldly desires, the energy can be transformed into productive qualities. On our way to finding the truth, we must ride our instincts. We must always keep in the light of the sun shining on our path, looking toward it as do the sunflowers. Always we must aim for the sun, whose gift is to endow us with maturity.

We have to reassess and change our values if we are to surmount our animal nature; only then can we begin to discern the clear spirit of our aim. Being still young, we are vulnerable to the wiles of the ego, which will seek to appropriate our zealousness for itself, to bolster its existence. We can easily be tempted by the strength of our impetuous nature to forget our aim. When this happens, we fall once more into our animal nature. Therefore we must seek to be vigilant, wakeful, in order to receive help from above, for we cannot proceed on our way to becoming balanced without its grace. The existence of this help should be constantly acknowledged in our minds. When we forget it, we are at the mercy of all the forces opposing our evolution, overcome by the sleep of the senses.

The forces of opposition are centered in our ego, giving rise to the strongest, yet entirely fictitious conviction that we are truly ourselves, thus constituting an implacable enemy to our essential selves. Only by seeing ego for what it is can its powers be diminished, and only by the growth of consciousness can we begin to realize that what is truly ourselves is of another order of being and must not be confused with ego. This begins to deprive the ego of its false meaning, the energy that nourishes its existence; but when threatened with starvation, it employs all its cunning to maintain its sustenance and strength. For example, it can easily tickle our vanity if for one moment we are inattentive and are blind to its ruses.

Soon, our sincerity, insight, understanding, and our will to practice what we have so far learned are going to be tested. The sun has shown us the brilliant world that can be ours. From now on the sun will be hidden by the night, through which we must pass by our own efforts. Provided we remember the vision vouchsafed to us and do not forget it, or lose trust in it, we shall not fail to overcome the difficulties. Strong faith is necessary.

# THE MOON

CONSCIOUS SUF-FERING AND voluntary labor must now be practiced. The night has closed over us, and no more having the sun's brilliance to show us the way, we have to develop our faculty of inner observation, so that it becomes more subtle and penetrating. We are going to cross the waters of life. Resisting its attractions, we nevertheless face life and learn what it is in every respect. With this knowledge we are armed against the danger of succumbing to its hypnotic lures.

The innocent child within us, our undeveloped essence, needs to grow up, to start to gain experience which will bring it to maturity. Although assisted by our increase of consciousness, he is alone against the forces exerting their powers to restrain him from growing up; that is to say, the forces in the subconscious. This lowest level of ourselves has to be recognized and acknowledged. It is represented on the card by a crab, which feeds on cor-

17

rupted matter. This is its mode of life; it is its being, in which it takes enjoyment.

The light of the moon, a borrowed light, gives an illusory appearance to our surroundings, and we may easily take them for what they are not. This light and its effects perturb people's minds, causing all kinds of creeping fears and crawling horrors. Taking the light of the moon for the real luminary of their intellectual, moral, and spiritual life, people dare not ask questions; they keep in their corners, in their towers. Only by remembering that we carry within us our own sunlight, and never forgetting it, can we be free of the influence of the moon.

Anyone who tries to liberate himself from the pull and illusions of nature will soon hear the chorus of the hounds, that is to say, they will be assailed by hostile criticisms and insults coming from people whose sense-based minds are sure that there is no other kind of truth, no other level of being than that with which they are identified. They will even show us "the scrolls" upon which their truths are written, as evidence of their absoluteness and as proof that there is nothing further to learn. They will do all in their power to dissuade us from undertaking our inner evolution. They will put all kinds of obstacles in our path, but nothing must deter us from our aim. This is the level ruled by materialism, inhabited by servile spirits, savage souls, creatures dragging their bodies along close to the ground, blind and deaf to life on a higher level. They seek security, each in his own invented "ivory tower" where he imagines he can protect himself from the world beyond. In their ignorance, conceit, vanity, pride, and hatreds they recoil against the idea of growth and expansion of being. They remain in their rigid, petty mentality. Although the way to their regeneration passes at the foot of their towers, they do not see it.

Nevertheless, our essence riding on its horse can meet this level of life without fear of its illusions if it learns how to be *in* life but not *of* it. Perhaps a touch of compassion may enter its heart for the first time, from its new experience and from understanding the horrifying situation into which these people have become fixed by mistaking the false light for the real.

# THE STAR

IT IS WRITTEN THAT WHEN YOU have found the beginning of the way, the stars will guide you.

After succeeding in passing through the night, the feminine principle—that is, the intuition—becomes stronger, for it has transcended the gravitational pull of the forces of nature.

The stars are the light by which our newly awakened awareness is guided. When, without covering our nakedness and remaining purified of the senses and their reactions, we have been tested and tempered by the night, the soul is able to meet life and grow. Later on it will become the seeker's guide to higher levels of spiritual illumination.

An incorruptible state of purity has to be maintained. This requires diligent meditation and work on ourselves. The truth of our discoveries will be poured on the earth of our being. From now on we are going to live by the truths revealed through our guiding light and no longer by the values of the world. We are beginning to differentiate between the qualities inherent in the levels of being below us and in those above us. Gradually the voice of Real Conscience is becoming audible. The further we move from our former selves, the more free of the false, acquired conscience is our being. Our new, regenerated life must henceforth be founded on Real Conscience. Meanwhile, until illumination has been received, our feminine intuition is our reliable support. We are alone, going toward the unknown, but bearing in our hearts the intimations that, when first received, moved us to start on our way.

This is a time for great concentration of attention and effort, of deep self-study, of endless perception of mistakes, how they arise and how they may be relinquished, and for the persistence of great faith. All these are necessary on the path. Our lives have to become symbolical tokens of rebirth. We are no longer working for material rewards and sensual satisfaction, but are undergoing all the experiences necessary for the tempering of our character as it keeps to the path of inner evolution. We are preparing ourselves to receive, and become the instruments of, the rays from above. Having stripped off the garments of passions and desires, they must not be resumed. Using our natural intelligence, aided by the radiant energies of the stars, we begin to understand the mysteries of nature, modifying our sensations and unfolding higher, more subtle inner senses and experiences.

The soul is not the instrument for dealing with life:

it is the vessel for receiving the forces from above, by which we learn how to stand on abstract ground, a strange experience after being so accustomed to the feel of the hard world of facts up till now.

The light that now is shed on our lives, although as yet dim, is immensely rewarding. It comes because we have begun to discard all our preconceived ideas and illusions.

# THE TOWER

WHEN WE HAVE SUFFICIENT self-knowledge, when, with the help of the soul, we have increased in strength, when the world ceases to be feared, when in endeavoring to discard our illusions and ignorance we have worked sincerely on ourselves, diligently and profoundly, then we are in the state that is ready to receive a great shock from above. It comes as the first intimation of the reality of illumination. Although just a corner of the sun shows itself, it is powerful enough to break up our ivory tower and set fire to its contents. This is the moment of the great downfall of our ego. All the many "I's" and all their facets in our personality are sent crashing to the ground. This is when we are tested to the full. All that we have imagined and believed ourselves to be is revealed, by the light from on high, as worth nothing. We are nothing. We realize that, in our ignorance, our beliefs and reasonings were false. We had built on "sand." The whole structure was no

23

more than a mass of superficial opinions, erroneous theories motivated by self-aggrandizement and self-will.

The flames which set fire to the tower and destroyed its contents have dual powers. As well as being destructive, they are the powers which transform our desires into sublime, spiritual impulses. Their light gives love and warmth. With our inner vision, our thoughts, and our motives directed always upward, our young will is exercised and increased in the practice of exercising it. Just as the phoenix is reborn from the ashes, so must our being be uplifted in the ascending flames. Have no fear of the conflagration; use its full potentiality in order to be carried upward. Fear would only destroy the soul and we would regress to being the Fool once more, with all his useless exaltation in material desires, blinded by the smoke of imagination.

Let us remember always to be like the sunflower, turned toward the sun, else will the negative forces of opposition overcome us. The further we ascend the path of regeneration the stronger becomes the opposition. This is continually to be borne in mind, and every situation is to be observed. As passive spectators of the destruction of the ego, we are thankful to have been given the strength to reach this stage.

# THE BLACK MAGICIAN

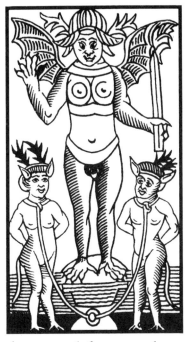

AFTER THE SHOCK OF SEE-ing our nothingness, and even though we may have directed our attention upward, a little of our imaginary personage remains. We are in a weak state and prone to doubts. This is the moment for which the dark forces are waiting.

Up till this stage we have gained ground gradually, but now we are face to face with the evils of our fallen nature. It is time to assess this earthly personality for better or for worse. We need the natural forces to keep us alive, physically, and our body is given to us with all its systems in working order. However, the characteristics of our personality have been acquired haphazardly and are in disorder. In order to gain our balance, these characteristics need to be observed and acknowledged before we can achieve harmony. For example, vanity must be moderated so that it can be transformed into dignity; our anger must be tamed into courage and energy; sloth must become rest from labor or preparation for action. We may earn what is necessary for our daily needs, but the accumulation of wealth from sheer greed is to be avoided. Envy of others only too easily incites us to emulate them; the indulgence of the senses results in over-sensuality.

The process of ordering and harmonizing our characteristics is not possible without understanding the truth and the good, the meaning and purpose of our aim. Daily our understanding is challenged; the habitual reactions to the forces of nature can easily recur, unless we will what we understand. By willing what we understand, the understanding grows and with it the will, in turn, increases. This requires constant valuation and mindfulness, so that we may be purged of any trace of insincerity, the devil being quick to notice fictitious superiority arising from any opinion we have of ourselves.

It is at this stage that we notice that the forces of our materialistic world are under the wings of the power of darkness. Stubbornness and obstinacy are the usual marks of the masses. It is a sign of the reversal of our understanding when we can acknowledge that we have been kept in bondage by the blind acceptance of the wrong values belonging to the powers of darkness, because we were ignorant of the powers of light. In the state of ignorance, our observations cannot but be superficial, and our reasoning false. Everything is referred to the level of the external senses but this does not prevent us from imagining that we are living far above it, such are our dreams of self-exaltation.

While we are only male and female, chained by our desires to the materialism of the lower forces of existence, our possibilities of development are limited by inertia and ignorance. When we realize the nature of the forces we have been under, when we face them and name them, a great calm accompanies the seeker on his way.

# TEMPERANCE

FROM ABOVE DE-SCENDS A VIVIFY-ing fluid, a new sap which is also the cleansing water of divine wisdom that washes away all our moral dirt. Thus regenerated, we are stronger, ready for the next stage of our journey, and freed from humankind's usual agitations. We can now remain serene amidst the turbulence, compassionate for mankind's weaknesses, secure against the pitfalls of life. Egoism and the passions are appeased. We are ready to re-enter life, renewed in vigor, light and gay in being, with an attitude that is disinterested and impassive, because we have come to terms with it. We can accept our tasks and fulfill them to the best of our ability.

Hitherto we were ruled by the laws of accident; anything could happen to us at any time, as is the lot of sleeping humanity. Now we are under a different law, that which governs our real being, our essence. Our guardian angel is starting to protect us; it is he who pours the divine fluid, the vital force, into our newly-cleansed vessel.

At this time it is probable that our life will take a new turning and what belongs to us by essential right comes to pass. Indeed, miracles may occur. Well aware of being guided from above, although to an unknown end, we receive prodigious gifts such that our faith is renewed, our willingness is strengthened and our enthusiasm for persisting is fired. Nothing, now, should hinder us from journeying further.

The energies of our animal nature being tamed, they become, by transformation, the force to assist us in the process of inner evolution. The rays of the sun no longer scorch us, nor does its fire burn us. The cooling waters of temperance refresh us on the way. The pendulum on which we swung between the positive and negative reactions to life has had its momentum decreased. Events can be taken in a calmer frame of mind, in a more equable mood. We can stand above the pettiness and miseries of life.

# DEATH–THE REAPER

THE MANY FACETS OF OUR EGO ARE now ready to be up-rooted. By mastering our passions and impulsiveness, our weaknesses cease to be indulged and nourished. Death is their lot and gladly do we accept the reaper who clears away the rubbish. All the multifarious fantasies rising from our imagination, fed by the day-dreams of ourselves, hindered our advance on the way. They must die so as to be succeeded by the creative imagination, by true spirituality. Accepting this death willingly and joyfully, the complete sacrifice of oneself, we are freed from all terrestrial imperfections.

Until now all the work on ourselves has been to overcome the power of the natural personality. By continuous and precise observation, by learning how to distinguish the wheat from the chaff, yet without judgement, by laying down pride and vanity the multitude of pictures of ourselves are humbled and brought down to earth, where they belong, where the scythe cuts through them. The importance with which we crowned ourselves is but nothing, and although it had, earlier, been shattered to the ground, it had not died. Nature is strong and always ready to bring its children to life, easily tempting us who are so weak as to play the Fool again.

The continual blows which have deflated our ego are exhausting, and if we had not received, between times, the gift of forces from above, we would have surrendered to the forces from below. We must remember that the further we go from our terrestrial selves, the stronger is the power of resistance brought against us by nature. As we develop, the tension between the two forces becomes stronger and stronger and can only be borne in true humility, realizing that without help from above we are but leaves tossed about by the winds of this earth, quite incapable of directing our steps, and no longer being convinced that we are in control. Things happened to us, by chance, by accident: we did not direct them. At best, we managed to deal with the situations by craftiness, but they still happened.

Now more than ever, having died to our personality, little of us remains. We are as a child lost in an unknown world and, like him, must commit ourselves to higher forces.

# THE HANGED MAN

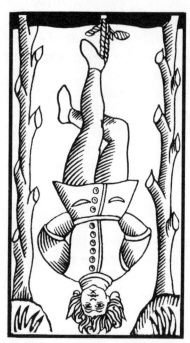

HAVING GIVEN UP THE EGO AND ITS self-will, we accept the will of the higher forces in humble obeisance; no longer do we work for results and rewards. Our only desire is for the sacrifice of ourselves and to serve the will of the mysterious power above. It is work for the work's sake. Our present stage has been reached through experiencing and learning from all the difficulties which have had to be met and transmuted. Our whole being radiates with the riches so abundantly gathered in our hearts, affecting our entire manner of life and our relationship with everyone. The gold of goodness and the silver of truth can be imparted to whoever is ready to receive these gifts.

When the sacrifice of the self is steadfast, it becomes clear that the individual human being is not developed enough to take charge of himself, though he imagines he can do as he pleases: in fact, he "does" nothing, his personality reacts according to its conditioned multiplicity of

# THE HANGED MAN

"I's." Only when we realize that such is our situation and are convinced that real mastery is possible, may we wish to undergo the transformation of being that will bring about our regeneration from the state of sleep to the state of full consciousness. If the wish is strong enough, then by devotion, disinterested and voluntary sacrifice of every idea and feeling of ourselves for the sake of what is higher than ourselves, this transformation will gradually be achieved.

Now that our aim is directed to the highest level of being, we accept being led by the soul, instead of being led by what we imagined to be our own will: it is the exact contrary, a reversal of our own way. In this sacrifice we know there is joy. We can smile and be happy, certain, by reason of the gifts already received, that what comes from above is good. Miseries, chaos, sickness, and violence only exist on the level of life where progress is seen as a vast expanse of materialism. At a higher level, above the clouds, there is peace. There the sun is always shining. It is the level where "Thy Will," and no more "my will," is done, and we start to feel and understand the power of this Will as it becomes stronger.

# THE ENCHANTRESS

## (FORCE—STRENGTH)

HERE IS THE FEMININE FORCE that tames the bestial, violent, male strength of the world. She has far transcended the level of the weak, imprisoned female completely under the power of nature, which she was in the beginning. At this stage, having dominated the instincts, these powers can be used as her servants. Until man has penetrated far enough inside himself to reach his intuitive strength, he will remain possessed by his brutish force and egoistic passions. He will be the eternal "Fool."

But at this stage on the way, after sacrificing our ego, the psychic energy is predominant. This enables us to calculate each further step wisely. We are in charge of our nature and can foresee the consequences of our behavior, which gives us the calm to be more careful. Our dealings with outer events and inner states have become much more intelligent. Our labors are undertaken with positive energy, for we know where we are going, in contrast to our ignorance and blindness when under the powers of natural life.

Our even temper and clear, transparent assurance can irradiate our surroundings, vivifying them with strength and joy. No longer do we feel any compulsion to impose or project our will upon them. Knowing how to behave in all situations, we can treat them with ease, uncomplicated by the usual behavior caused by the reactions of the ego.

We start to see through the substance of life and are not lured by its enticements and false offerings, as we were previously. Rather than wasting energy, we can now control the expenditure of energy given to any one situation. Being in a higher level of oneself, we experience a much faster rate of taking in impressions, thereby giving us a more comprehensive view of the external and internal worlds and preparing us to meet circumstances in the appropriate way. Being detached, we are not glued by the senses to life-situations. Problems that seem big when, so to speak, we have our nose against them, are but small and light when met in an objective state of consciousness. When we know how to master ourselves, we can be master of all situations; the possibilities are tremendous and likewise is the temptation to use this power for our own purposes. We must remain humble and willing servants of the higher powers we have now received. Were we to use them for ourselves, though all might seem well for a time, they would become destructive. It must not be forgotten that the forces of darkness are always waiting to seize this energy, should there be any failure on our part as its guardian. Temptation is always present: we must be awake and vigilant to recognize and withstand it. Vital energy must be transformed into salutary strength. Lead must be transmuted into gold. The spirit is dominating matter.

# THE WHEEL
# OF FORTUNE

IN A STATE OF DE-
TACHMENT THE
wheel of eternal recur-
rence which brings the ups
and downs of everyday life
can be watched. It is seen
that everything is twofold;
darkness and light, strength
and weakness, joy and sorrow, life and death, et cetera,
et cetera. Never for a moment
does the cosmic wheel stay
still. We are carried on it in
perpetual motion, willy-
nilly, one moment going up,
one moment going down. It
is pathetic to watch people
in a state of excitement, full
of energy and enthusiasm when their lives appear to be
prospering, when at last good luck seems to be attending
them. They are being carried upward by the momentum
of the wheel, unaware that on reaching its zenith the turn
of the wheel inevitably will carry them downwards. This
is the way of the Fool. He is governed by chance, by the
hazardous nature of life, and is forever insecure in an
always unstable situation. Without a supreme effort to

detach ourselves from it, we remain on this wheel, ever at its mercy.

On attaining control of our passions and desires, the turning wheel bringing its good or bad opportunities can be watched objectively. By now we have gained a certain ability to discriminate and to be alert to recognize and seize the opportunity offered in each present moment. But we must be swift to act, for opportunities pass quickly and are hardly discernible, for the most part. It is a very subtle game, and more often than not we are left regretting the opportunities that we have missed. When we can see what is being given at any one time destiny is propitious. It can bring luck without any personal merit attaching to it.

The joy, the sense of well-being and enthusiasm now experienced, are not attributed blindly to ourselves, but are realized, with awe and thankfulness, as being radiated from above. This radiant power is very strong and must not be wasted. With a cool head we have to be in control of it and ready to cut away with the sword of discrimination any evil that may appear. This vital radiation can enable us to grow and to resist the destructive agents of the world. The aim is to gain perfect equilibrium, to win freedom from endless recurrences, liberation from the wheel of reincarnation.

It is a state of understanding, of valuation. We are strong enough now to take the initiative for a *higher* purpose.

# THE HERMIT

HAVING RE-MAINED SEPA-rated from the mechanically induced moods, between being now up and now down, we enter into a greater depth in ourselves. Quietly we stay outside the bustle of this world. Being in it, but no more of it, we are no longer influenced by it. We can continue on our way tranquilly, without haste, carrying our own light. Though, compared to the sunlight, it is not very bright, it is our own, made by our own efforts. Step by step looking for the truth in concentration and meditation, in contrast with the Fool who wants immediate rewards for all he does, we are working without any wish for praise. In modesty, without any illusion as to our knowledge, we realize how little we know in comparison with that of which we are ignorant. It is with profound humility that we harvest the fruits of our work, in order to continue our terrestrial task. We are travelling into our own darkness, the subconscious. To have full knowledge of ourselves, it is as important to learn what is at the deepest interior levels as it is to learn about our exterior self and what lies on the surface.

Though by now we have somewhat matured, a staff is still needed to help our steps in the darkness. We have to work alone, well cloaked, protected from the external world and the power of evil. The higher truths we are learning must be hidden from ordinary ears, for they are too powerful for people not prepared to hear them. It needs the long initiation of the way in order to become ready to bear them. Therefore we must remain silent. We must perform our daily tasks well and skillfully, in contact with people, while sealing our selves hermetically and not feeding on trivialities. Our aim requires us to concentrate our thoughts deeply if we are to reach the mystical and perfect equilibrium.

# JUSTICE

ALL WORDLY AM-BITIONS HAV-ing been abandoned, and having put our feet on the holy path, our soul is now in charge and guiding our steps. There is a definite change of consciousness: it is as if we are entering a vast, more brilliant world. All the variations of moods with which we were mechanically identified no longer affect us, nor do we hesitate to continue on our way. A great strength has entered our hearts. It is an inner, emotional force which provides an enormous psychological power of Wisdom and Understanding, on the level of positive, real emotion, distinct from the emotions which the natural man experiences in his ordinary life.

We are now in a world of revelation, giving us the qualities of integrity, the capacity for love and courage, charity and discrimination. Our soul is poised between Mercy and Judgement, warmth and severity. The eyes are open: justice is no longer blindfolded. Things and people are seen with great clarity and strict impartiality. We have become fully responsible for our actions, over which we are able to exercise control. Should we fail to act properly when certain requests are made to us we know we have missed the mark, have "sinned," and that we are not forgiven. We are approaching spiritual adulthood and are expected to know how to behave in all circumstances and deal with all manner of events. The sword of spiritual combativeness cuts away our every weakness. We are no more under the ordinary laws of accident which govern the worldy personality, but have come under the law governing our essential self, the law of fate. It is time to stop repeating the useless, mechanical pattern of thought and conduct: there must be no regression, no falls, no stumblings.

By now the woman has cultivated her intellect and uses it with assurance. She uses it logically, honestly, with integrity, discipline and surety of judgement. She can take decisions, make firm resolves confident of where she is going. The man, in addition to his masculine attributes, has opened himself to his feminine side, which brings him warmth of heart, compassion, and charity. The masculine and feminine sides of ourselves can combine harmoniously. Real conscience rules.

# THE CHARIOT

NOW BEING IN CONTROL OF ourselves, we can take charge of the vehicle of our being and direct it through life, instead of it being tossed about by life.

We have gained strength enough to harness the tremendous energies emitted by our wordly desires, by our animal passions, and by the forces of opposition. Once these are harnessed, they must be controlled from within our vehicle of being, but at first we find these forces pulling in different directions, testing our patience, our composure and our humility. Should we become over-confident at this juncture, or self-congratulatory, the Fool immediately takes over and drives the horses straight for the precipice. This is why we must never cease to remind ourselves to keep quietly and humbly within ourselves. Even at this stage we have no will of our own. We are being guided by the soul and, in turn, we are guiding the horses. We are apprentice-drivers, though potentially in a victorious position. We are as if learning to sail, at first on a lake or close in to the seashore, before gradually going out further and further on the ocean.

Hitherto the events of life had merely happened to us, but we have been learning how to take all the kicks and shocks as lessons which can be clearly seen and dealt with. For purposes of higher development we have to guide ourselves through events which may never have been encountered were we to have remained on a lower level of being. We know in what we are lacking and endeavor to remedy our deficiencies. No undertaking should remain neglected or only partly fulfilled. Life must no longer be our master; we must master life. The soul knows what we need and guides us to it. Our progress becomes a conscious process, our evolution becomes intelligent, and our spirituality becomes active. By understanding ourselves, we understand life and so are able to drive about in it with tact and discernment, peacefully in harmony with it. At this stage the soul, being in command, guides us to the throne of the spirit.

# THE LOVERS

THE TRIALS OF LIFE HAVE POLished our roughness and transformed our violence. Every single thing and person are seen by the brilliant light of the full sun. Our hearts are being filled with a vast love for the world and for humanity. True compassion, in its real sense, is possessing us, and love, in a higher, mature form, unlike the sentimental, immature love on the earthly level, has entered us. Being no more imprisoned in nature, we are able to understand it in a new way, and at one with our surroundings, we have a marvelous appreciation of nature's beauty, its gifts and healing powers, in our hearts. We are sorry for the arrogant male vandals who, in their blindness, ignorance, and foolishness, are destroying nature's gifts. The forces of darkness continue on their process of ruination, but if we exert ourselves so as not to be identified with them, we gain the opportunity to direct their power upward, to lift us to higher levels of

45

being within ourselves, instead of being carried downward. For we have learned that the transformation of our life consists in transforming our impressions of it. We can but weep for the Fool going on his way to destruction: though the path to higher development is ever present, he does not take it, and there is nothing we can do about it.

As we are now in contact with our soul, we should allow it to be our guide, for its knowledge, perception, and understanding are greater than ours. We are still but students of love: nevertheless, we are wide open to this warm and brilliant light above us. From the trials of life, we have learned the value of everything and know how useless it is to crave for more and more material possessions to support our ego. Consequently we are living as simply as possible, amidst nature, working with it diligently, and not against it, loving it for all its lavish gifts. We have all we require. Our task is to prepare our being to be fit to re-enter the lost garden, Eden. Nothing was lacking there, but once the quality of love was separated from man, he fell to a very low level of being. He must be regenerated by the woman's love and patience, and also, at this stage, by her firmness. She, being the principle of mature love, must take the initiative and act.

It is woman's turn to renew our surroundings and relationships before it is too late. She can bring warmth, peace, enjoyment of the gifts of nature, creativity, and beauty. She can imbue us with the sense of responsibility for our humanness. Yet each of us has to undertake the transformation of our being individually, not waiting upon someone else to do this for us. Each of us has to attain to the highest level within us, passing through all levels, by hard, incessant, yet rewarding work. The attractions of life are subtle and insidious, but we are now able to recognize its tricks. Moreover, having values superior to life's attractions, we are immune to them.

Love for the highest qualities of being and compassion for the lowest is the finest state which a human can reach in his heart. The tremendous suffering and sorrow which mankind brings on itself are clearly seen and understood. Darkness is heavy and pulls us down, while lightness lifts us up into the luminous clarity of consciousness where things can be seen, apprehended, and loved.

# THE HIEROPHANT

SELFLESS LOVE HAS OPENED THE door to the understanding of mystical love. The moral laws of every religion have to be known and comprehended, so that it can be seen that all the great religions are saying the same things, in different terms.

This is the stage where everything is seen from a level above that on which they occur. The ego has been superseded, and consequently nothing is done for a worldly purpose. All our actions are motivated by a higher aim. Our behavior has to radiate positive and loving energies toward others and permeate the manner in which we touch all things and in which we act. We are in a state of detachment: success or failure, joy or sorrow, the ups and downs of life, are equal. All the contraries are recognized as aspects of the pendulum on which life swings. In our state of blissful peace we are no longer affected by the rapid changes of moods and events. We are qualified to teach how to attain this new awareness to those who have ears to hear and eyes to see.

We have given up exerting what we called our own will and have accepted the will of the spirit as our guide in mastering our personal feelings. It now becomes possible to be imbued with goodness and affability, intuitiveness and contemplativeness, on the way to surrendering ourselves to the Sacred Mystery.

The spiritual crown is our right, but has to be earned by ceaseless work on the transformation of our being. Only someone of fully developed being can support the responsibility of this crown. Anyone lesser would be destroyed by the power brought by so great a knowledge and illumination. He who has the crown has reached the highest level in temporal, exoteric knowledge and the highest level in timeless, esoteric knowledge. He is now about to be immersed in the Love of God and in sanctity.

# THE EMPEROR

THE MAN HAS NOW ACHIEVED his full potentialities. He is no more dominated by life; he dominates it. His most noble aspirations can flower into the highest idealism and assure him of dominion in the sphere of human thought.

His thrusting, masculine, expansive action conduces to his coordination, to his methodical linking up of things, to strength, exactitude, positive actions, straightforwardness, and absolute certitude. Throughout his long apprenticeship he has been tested and tempered. Although making mistakes and suffering from them, he has always advanced with patience and fortitude, never giving up. He has grown in wisdom and caliber. He can recognize, at a glance, what is true and what is false. He is able to act appropriately, with dispassionate judgment, in both worldly and spiritual matters. He can govern the earth, his own nature, while being himself governed by the spirit. He has entered into himself and is no more subject to inner and outer conflicts. His will is pure and disinterested. He has transcended violence and is now in peace and harmony with his feminine side to which he is truly wedded. Both sides of himself are on the same level, fully complementing one another, although the man and the woman, outwardly, while still on earth, remain separate. Yet, instead of their original misunderstanding of one another, they are fully initiated into the mysteries of life and death, joy and suffering, through the hard experiences each has undergone.

Man can accomplish his task with the highest intelligence and in true royalty, as is his birth right. As his power is great and mighty, he must humbly recognize and acknowledge that he is under the authority of the spirit. Should he fail to remember this, the powers and energies with which he has been endowed will turn (as they can at each stage) into their opposites; that is, they will become tyrannical, absolute, hard, and violent. Once more he would become the Fool.

This is why the Fool is not numbered in the Tarot. He can take any number, for he can enter at any stage of our development if we are not on the alert.

# THE EMPRESS

THE WOMAN, HERE, HAS reached her full maturity: she is completely regenerated. She has control of her nature and is no more affected by the pull of the moon. She has dominion over all that is unstable, all that is in motion and capricious. The water of life, of consciousness, is flowing by. Though she is in nature, she is above it, having freed herself of the chains by which she was attached to it. Now she can hold the royal symbols of universal domination. Her intelligence is creative. She is suffused with beauty, serenity, purity, selflessness, dignity. Her interior life is vivid. Through transforming her impressions of outer circumstances, she understands their meaning at a higher level. Her devotion to truth is her strength.

Being in harmony and balance with her masculine side, she is a true spouse. The dissolution of terrestrial desires has released the energy to concentrate on the sublimification of the soul's harmony. There is full understanding of the man, just as the man fully understands the woman. It is a perfect union.

She can receive the crown of royalty and, being equal with her spouse, rule together with him. There is no separation between them. They are unified and directed by the same law. Fully knowing her role as woman, she will take responsibility for it and not impinge on the man's. When necessity arises for it, she will use her masculine development, as the man will use his feminine intuition when the situation calls for it. Each being the true servant of the Higher, neither will act out of turn. Each has an individual role, to which they are true.

It is only at the level of perfectly balanced harmony and love that they can, in unity, pass through the last stage of human growth to become divine: the return to the source, the re-entry into Eden.

# THE HIGH PRIESTESS

WHAT BETTER WORDS THAN those of Jacob Boehme in his *Three Principles* can be used to describe the sublime achievement of the feminine principle, through which everything must pass, ascending or descending the scale of being:

"Wisdom, the eternal virgin, the playmate of God to His honor and joy, becomes full of desire to behold the wonders of God that are contained within herself. Owing to this desire, the divine essences within her become active and attract the holy power and thus she enters into a state of permanent being. By this she does not conceive of anything within herself; her inclination is resting in the Holy Spirit. She merely moves before God for the purpose of revealing the wonders of God."

Having attained the supreme virtue through knowledge and experience, she is no more under the power of the world. This is the blissful state of unity, where no sense of otherness and no distinctions of sex exist. The soul reigns supreme; indeed, she is the soul. It is the supreme height of divine wisdom and perfection, total and final. She is poised between the pillars of opposite forces, as we have seen from the Balance, or the card for Justice. However, this time the next step is hidden by a veil concealing the Holy of Holies, wherein hovers the Divine Presence.

Only the Perfects will be able to pass through the veil, those who have attained to the last step at the top of the ladder of ascent. Only such ones by their preparation can withstand the immense shock on passing through the veil. Only the feminine principle in them can perform this task, as it involves the passive, receiving quality being pulled upward from above by the active principle as it thrusts itself into its pure openness. Then the will of the Spirit will gather these into its bosom.

This is the Gate of Eden, regained, where mankind purged of all its faults will be re-integrated in true stature.

Beyond the veil the Will of God is direct. As long as duality still persisted, it could not be faced. Only when united with the feminine principle can we pass through the veil and see God face to face.

# THE MAGICIAN

THE ULTIMATE STEP IS NOW reached. There is no longer our "own" personality and no longer a will of our own. Real will is acting through us. We are a channel for the Love of God.

Having passed through all degrees of initiation, we are at last able to "do": that is to say, we are skillful in all things, we have mastered the elements, we have perfected our understanding and can grasp what is willed of us from above. Thus, we can perform our task which, unlike what we have thought it to be, is to "Let Thy Will be done."

At certain periods in the world's history a teacher is sent, for reasons exactly beyond us, to teach mankind how to regenerate itself. Because he comes from the level of "The Son of God," he is able to accomplish the work appointed him, being directly under the Will of God. As an instrument of so great a power, he is able to make a tremendous impact in a short time: there is no need for him to stay long on earth. Indeed, he administers an enormous, deliberate shock to human beings to shake them out of their slumber and darkness. This shock has to sound all the way down the octave of creation, to inspire the very lowest level with hope. Those ready to receive it will respond and start to climb the ladder of being. In turn, they will succeed in reaching the level of the skillful Magician and will do the Will of God.

The sound of the shock is continually resounding; the trumpet is always blasting; the sun is always shining; the river of life is always flowing; the crown is ever ready for us to wear. We are the children of God, truly royal. The crown is our birth right, but it cannot be attained without our voluntary and conscious effort under the guidance of the ever-present teachings. These must be followed, rather than the incredible ideas we have of ourselves, in our arrogance and vanity imagining we know all that there is to be known.

At the "Magic" level there are no dualities, no sufferings, no sorrows, no violence and none of the plagues of mankind. Unlike the Fool who remains an innocent and immature youth, we, once developed to the full stature for which we were created, are restored to our *Eternal Youth* in the full Glory of the Creator.

This book was set in Benedictine, a linotype face developed from the types of Plato de Benedictis. Characterized by pure classic design, the type preserves the feeling of the inscriptions that beautify the Roman architecture of classic and Renaissance periods. The lower case gets its essential features from the medieval use of the quill pen in writing manuscript books.

*Composed by the Monotype Composition Company, Baltimore, Maryland.*
*Printed and bound by Thomson-Shore Inc.. Ann Arbor, Michigan.*
*Designed by Julia Runk.*